William Morris
After the painting by Watts.

LITTLE
JOURNEYS
to the Homes of
ENGLISH
AUTHORS
William Morris
Written by ELBERT
HUBBARD and done
into a Printed Book by
the ROYCROFTERS at
their Shop, which is in
EAST AURORA, Erie
Co., New York, U. S. A.
A. D. 1900

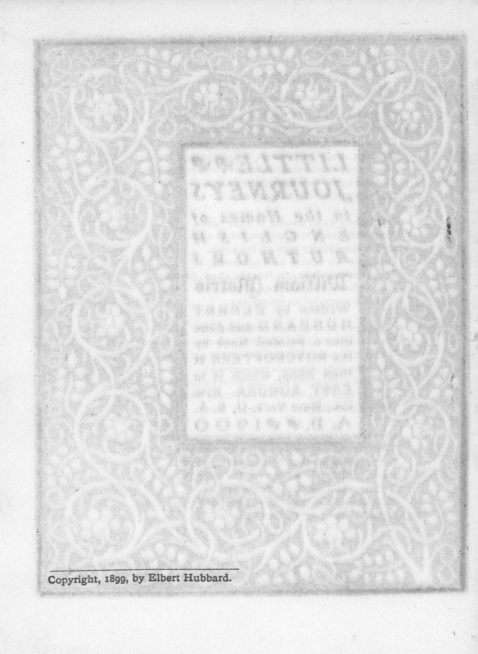

THE IDLE SINGER.

From "The Earthly Paradise."

Of Heaven or Hell I have no power to sing,
I cannot ease the burden of your fears,
Or make quick-coming death a little thing,
Or bring again the pleasure of past years,
Nor for my words shall ye forget your tears,
Or hope again for aught that I can say,
The idle singer of an empty day.

But rather, when aweary of your mirth,
From full hearts still unsatisfied ye sigh,
And feeling kindly unto all the earth,
Grudge every minute as it passes by,
Made the more mindful that the sweet days die,—
Remember me a little then, I pray,
The idle singer of an empty day.

The heavy trouble, the bewildering care
That weighs us down who live and earn our bread,
These idle verses have no power to bear,
So let me sing of names remembered,
Because they, living not, can ne'er be dead,
Or long time take their memory quite away
From a poor singer of an empty day.

Dreamer of dreams, born out of my due time,
Why should I strive to set the crooked straight?
Let it suffice me that my murmuring rhyme
Beats with light wing against the ivory gate,
Telling a tale not too importunate
To those who in the sleepy region stay,
Lulled by the singer of an empty day.

WILLIAM MORRIS

HE parents of William Morris were well-to-do people who lived in the village of Walthamstow, Essex. The father was a London bill-broker, cool-headed, calculating, practical. In the home of his parents William Morris received small impulse in the direction of art; he, however, was taught how to make both ends meet, and there were drilled into his character many good lessons of plain common sense—a rather unusual equipment for a poet, but still one that should not be waived nor considered lightly. At the village school William was neither precocious nor dull, neither black nor white: his cosmos being simply a sort of slaty-gray, which attracted no special attention from schoolfellows or tutors. From the village school he went to Marlborough Academy, where by patient grubbing he fitted himself for Exeter College, Oxford.

Morris the elder, proved his good sense by taking no very special interest in the boy's education. Violence of direction in education falls flat:

I

WILLIAM MORRIS man is a lonely creature, and has to work out his career in his own way. To help the grub spin its cocoon is quite unnecessary, and to play the part of Mrs. Gamp with the butterfly in its chrysalis stage, is to place a quietus upon its career. The whole science of modern education is calculated to turn out a good, fairish, commonplace article; but the formula for a genius remains a secret with Deity. The great man becomes great in spite of teachers and parents; and his near kinsmen, being color-blind, usually pooh-pooh the idea that he is anything more than mediocre.

❧ At Oxford, William Morris fell in with a young man of about his own age by the name of Edward Burne-Jones. Burne-Jones was studying theology. He was slender in stature, dreamy, spiritual, poetic. Morris was a giant in strength, blunt in speech, bold in manner, and had a shock of hair like a lion's mane. This was in the year 1853—these young men being nineteen years of age. The slender, yellow, dreamy student of theology and the ruddy athlete became fast friends ✂✂✂

"Send your sons to college and the boys will educate them," said Emerson. These boys read poetry together; and it seems the first author that specially attracted them was Mrs. Browning; & she attracted them simply because she had recently eloped with the man she loved. This fact proved to Morris that she was a worthy woman and a discerning. She had the courage of his convictions. To elope with a poor poet, leaving a rich

2

father and a luxurious home—what nobler ambition?
❧ Burne-Jones, student of theology, considered her
action proof of depravity. Morris, in order to show his
friend that Mrs. Browning was really a rare and gentle
soul, read aloud to Burne-Jones from her books. Morris himself had never read much of Mrs. Browning's
work, but in championing her cause and interesting
his friend in her, he grew interested himself. Like
lawyers, we undertake a cause first and look for proof
later. In teaching another, Morris taught himself. By
explaining a theme it becomes luminous to us.

In passing, it is well to note that this impulse in the
heart of William Morris to come to the defense of an
accused person was ever very strong. His defense of
Mrs. Browning led straight to "The Defense of Guinevere," begun while at Oxford and printed in book
form in his twenty-fourth year. Not that the offenses
of Guinevere and Elizabeth Barrett were parallel, but
Morris was by nature a defender of women. And it
should further be noted that Tennyson had not yet
written his "Idylls of the King," at the time Morris
wrote his poetic brief.

Another author that these young men took up at this
time was Ruskin. John Ruskin was fifteen years older
than Morris—an Oxford man, too,—also the son of a
merchant and rich by inheritance. Ruskin's natural
independence, his ability for original thinking and his
action in embracing the cause of Turner, the ridiculed,
won the heart of Morris. In Ruskin he found a

3

WILLIAM MORRIS writer who expressed the thoughts that he believed. He read Ruskin, and insisted that Burne-Jones should. Together they read " The Nature of Gothic," and then they went out upon the streets of Oxford & studied examples at first hand. They compared the old with the new, & came to the conclusion that the buildings erected two centuries before had various points to recommend them which modern buildings have not. The modern buildings were built by contractors, while the old ones were constructed by men who had all the time there was, and so they worked out their conceptions of the eternal fitness of things.

Then these young men, with several others, drew up a remonstrance against "the desecration by officious restoration, & the tearing down of time-mellowed structures to make room for the unsightly brick piles of boarding-house keepers."

The remonstrance was sent in to the authorities, and by them duly pigeon-holed, with a passing remark that young fellows sent to Oxford to be educated would better attend to their books and mind their own business. Having espoused the cause of the Middle Ages in architecture, these young men began to study the history of the people who lived in the olden time. They read Spenser and Chaucer, and chance threw in their way a dog-eared copy of Malory's " Morte D' Arthur," & this was still more dog-eared when they were through with it. Probably no book ever made more of an impression on Morris than this one; & if he had written

4

an article for the "Ladies' Home Journal" on "Books that Influenced Me Most," he would have placed Malory's "Morte D' Arthur " first.

The influence of Burne-Jones on Morris was marked, and the influence of Morris on Burne-Jones was profound. Morris discovered himself in explaining things to Burne-Jones, and Burne-Jones, without knowing it, adopted the opinions of Morris; and it was owing to Morris that he gave up theology.

Having abandoned the object that led him to college, Burne-Jones lost faith in Oxford, and went down to London to study art.

Morris hung on, secured his B. A. and articled himself to a local architect with the firm intent of stopping the insane drift for modern mediocrity, and bringing about a just regard for the stately dignity of the Gothic.

A few months' experience, however, and he discovered that an apprentice to an architect was not expected to furnish plans nor even criticise those already made: his business was to make detailed drawings from completed designs for the contractors to work from.

A year at architecture, with odd hours filled in at poetry and art, and news came from Burne-Jones that he had painted a picture, and sold it for ten pounds.

Now Morris had all the money he needed. His father's prosperity was at flood, & he had but to hint for funds and they came, yet to make things with your own hands and sell them, was the true test of success.

He had written "Gertha's Lovers," "The Tale of the

Hollow Land," and various poems and essays for the college magazines; & his book, " The Defense of Guinevere," had been issued at his own expense, and the edition was on his hands—a weary weight.

Thoreau wrote to his friends, when the house burned and destroyed all copies of his first book, " The edition is exhausted," but no such happiness came to Morris. And so when glad tidings of an artistic success came from Burne-Jones, he resolved to follow the lead and abandon architecture for "pure art."

Arriving in London he placed himself under the tutorship of Dante Gabriel Rossetti, poet, dreamer & artist, six years his senior, whom he had known for some time, and who had also instructed Burne-Jones.

While taking lessons in painting at the rather shabby house of Rossetti in Portland Street, he was introduced to Rossetti's favorite model—a young woman of rare grace and beauty. Rossetti had painted her picture as "TheBlessedDamozel," leaning over the bar of Heaven, while the stars in her hair were seven. Morris the impressionable fell in love with the canvas and then with the woman.

When they were married, tradition has it, that Rossetti withheld his blessing & sought to drown his sorrow in fomentations, with dark, dank hints in baritone to the effect that the Thames only could appreciate his grief.

But grief is transient; and for many years Rossetti and Burne-Jones pictured the tall, willowy figure of Mrs.

6

Morris as the dream-woman, on tapestry and canvas; and as the "Blessed Virgin," her beautiful face and form are shown in many sacred places.

Truth need not be distorted in a frantic attempt to make this an ideal marriage—only a woman with the intellect of Minerva could have filled the restless heart of William Morris. But the wife of Morris believed in her lord, and never sought to hamper him; and if she failed at times to comprehend his genius, it was only because she was human.

Whistler once remarked that without Mrs. Morris to supply stained-glass attitudes and the lissome beauty of an angel, the Pre-Raphaelites would have long since gone down to dust and forgetfulness.

THE year which William Morris spent at architecture, he considered as nearly a waste of time, but it was not so in fact. As a draughtsman he had developed a marvelous skill, and the grace and sureness of his lines were a delight to Burne-Jones, Rossetti, Holman Hunt, Ford Madox Brown and others of the little artistic circle in which he found himself. Youth lays great plans; youth is always in revolt against the present order; youth groups itself in bands and swears eternal fealty; and life, which is change, dissipates the plans, subdues the revolt into conformity,

WILLIAM MORRIS and the sworn friendships fade away into dull indifference. Always? Well, no, not exactly. In this instance the plans and dreams found form; the revolt was a revolution that succeeded; & the brotherhood existed for near fifty years, and then was severed only by death ᕊᕚᕊ

Without going into a history of the Pre-Raphaelite Brotherhood, it will be noted that the band of enthusiasts in art, literature & architecture had been swung by the arguments and personality of William Morris into the strong current of his own belief, and this was that Art and Life in the Middle Ages were much lovelier things than they are now.

That being so, we should go back to medieval times for our patterns. A study of the best household decoration of the Fifteenth Century showed that all the furniture used then was made to fit a certain apartment, and with a definite purpose in view. Of course it was made by hand, and the loving marks of the tool were upon it ❧ It was made as good and strong and durable as it could be made. Floors & walls were of mosaic or polished wood, and these were partially covered by beautifully woven rugs, skins & tapestries. The ceilings were sometimes ornamented with pictures painted in harmony with the use for which the room was designed. Certainly there were no chromos, and the pictures were few and these of the best, for the age was essentially a critical one.

A modest circular was issued in which the fact was

made known that, "A company of historical artists will use their talents in home decoration." Dealers into whose hands this circular fell, smiled in derision, and the announcement made no splash in England's artistic waters. But the leaven was at work which was bound to cause a revolution in the tastes of fifty million people.

Most of our best moves are accidents, and every good thing begins as something else. In the beginning there was no expectation of building up a trade or making a financial success of the business. The idea was simply that the eight young men who composed the band were to use their influence in helping each other to secure commissions, and corroborate the views of doubting patrons as to what was art and what not. In other words, they were to stand by each other. Ford Madox Brown, Dante Gabriel Rossetti, Burne-Jones and Arthur Hughes were painters; Philip Webb an architect; Peter Paul Marshall a landscape gardener and engineer; Charles Joseph Faulkner, an Oxford don, was a designer, and William Morris was an all 'round artist—ready to turn his hand to anything. These men undertook to furnish a home from garret to cellar in an artistic way.

Work came & each set himself to help all the others. From simply supplying designs for furniture, rugs, carpets and wall paper they began to manufacture these things, simply because they could not buy or get others to make the things they desired.

WILLIAM MORRIS Morris undertook the entire executive charge of affairs, and mastered the details of half a dozen trades in order that he might intelligently conduct the business. The one motto of the firm was, "Not how cheap, but how good." They insisted that housekeeping must be simplified, and that we should have fewer things and have them better. To this end single pieces of furniture were made and all sets of furniture discarded. I have seen several houses furnished entire by William Morris, and the first thing that impressed me was the sparsity of things. Instead of a dozen pictures in a room, there were two or three—one on an easel and one or two on the walls ✗ Gilt frames were abandoned almost entirely and dark stained woods were used instead. Wide fireplaces were introduced & mantels of solid oak. For upholstery, leather covering was commonly used instead of cloth. Carpets were laid in strips, not tacked down to stay, and rugs were laid so as to show a goodly glimpse of hard-wood floor; and in the dining room a large round table was placed instead of a right angle square one. This table was not covered with a table-cloth; mats and doilies being used here and there. To cover a table entire with a cloth or spread, was pretty good proof that the piece of furniture was cheap and shabby; so in no William Morris library or dining room would you find a table entirely covered. The round dining table is in very general use now, but few people realize how its plainness was scouted when William Morris first introduced it.

One piece of William Morris furniture has become de- cidedly popular in America, and that is the "Morris Chair." The first chair of this pattern was made entirely by the hands of the master. It was built by a man who understood anatomy, unlike most chairs and all church pews. It was also strong, durable, ornamental and by a simple device the back could be adjusted so as to fit a man's every mood.

❦ There has been a sad degeneracy among William Morris chairs; still, good ones can be obtained, nearly as excellent as the one in which I rested at Kelmscott House—broad, deep, massive, upholstered with curled hair, and covered with leather that would delight a book-binder. Such a chair can be used a generation and then passed on to the heirs.

Furnishing of churches and chapels led naturally to the making of stained glass windows, and hardly a large city of Christendom but has an example of the Morris work ❦ ❦

Morris managed to hold that erratic genius, Dante Gabriel Rossetti, in line and direct his efforts, which of itself was a feat worthy of record. He made a fortune for Rossetti, who was a child in this world's affairs, and he also made a fortune for himself and every man connected with the concern.

Burne-Jones stood by the ship manfully and proved his good sense by never interfering with the master's plans, or asking foolish, quibbling questions,—showing faith on all occasions.

II

WILLIAM MORRIS The Morris designs for wall paper, tapestry, cretonnes and carpets are now the property of the world, but to say just which is a William Morris design and which a Burne-Jones is an impossibility, for these two strong men worked together as one being with two heads and four hands. At one time, I find the firm of Morris & Co. had three thousand hands at work in its various manufactories, the work in most instances being done by hand and after the manner of the olden time ⚜ William Morris was an avowed socialist long before so many men began to grow fond of calling themselves Christian Socialists. Morris was too practical not to know that the time is not ripe for life on a communal basis, but in his heart was a high and holy ideal that he has partially explained in his books, "A Dream of John Ball" and "News from Nowhere," and more fully in many lectures. His sympathy was ever with the workingman and those who grind fordone at the wheel of labor. To better the condition of the toiler was his sincere desire. But socialism to him was more of an emotion than a well worked out plan of life. He believed that men should replace competition by Co-operation. He used to say, "I'm going your way, so let us go hand in hand. You help me and I'll help you. We shall not be here very long, for soon, Death, the kind old nurse, will come and rock us all to sleep—let us help one another while we may." And that is about the extent of the socialism of William Morris. There is one criticism that has been constantly brought

12

against Morris, and although he answered this criticism a thousand times during his life, it still springs
fresh—put forth by little men who congratulate themselves on having scored a point.

❧ They ask in orotund, "How could William Morris
expect to benefit society at large, when all of the
products he manufactured were so high in price that
only the rich could buy them?"
Socialism, according to William Morris, does not con-
sider it desirable to supply cheap stuff to anybody. The
socialist aims to make every manufactured article of
the best quality possible. It is not how cheap can this
be made, but how good. Make it as excellent as it can
be made to serve its end. Then sell it at a price that
affords something more than a bare subsistence to the
workmen who put their lives into its making. In
this way you raise the status of the worker—you pay
him for his labor and give him an interest and pride in
the product. Cheap products make cheap men. The first
thought of socialism is for the worker who makes the
thing, not the man who buys it.
Work is for the worker.
What becomes of the product of your work, and how
the world receives it, matters little. But how you do
it is everything. We are what we are on account of
the thoughts we have thought and the things we have
done. As a muscle grows strong only through use, so
does every attribute of the mind, and every quality of
the soul take on new strength through exercise. And

WILLIAM MORRIS on the other hand, as a muscle not used atrophies and dies, so will the faculties of the spirit die through disuse ✗✗✗

Thus we see why it is very necessary that we should exercise our highest and best. We are making character—building soul-fibre; and no rotten threads must be woven into this web of life. If you write a paper for a learned society, you are the man who gets the benefit of that paper—the society may. If you are a preacher and prepare your sermons with care, you are the man who receives the uplift—and as to the congregation, it is all very doubtful.

Work is for the worker.

We are all working out our own salvation. And thus do we see how it is very plain that John Ruskin was right when he said that the man who makes the thing is of far more importance than the man who buys it. Work is for the worker.

Can you afford to do slip-shod, evasive, hypocritical work? Can you afford to shirk, or make-believe or practice pretence in any act of life? No, no, for all the time you are molding yourself into a deformity, and drifting away from the Divine. What the world does and says about you is really no matter, but what you think and what you do are questions vital as fate. No one can harm you but yourself. Work is for the worker. ✗ And so I will answer the question of the critics as to how society has been benefited by, say, a William Morris book:

14

1.—The workmen who made it found a pride and satisfaction in their work.

2.—They received a goodly reward in cash for their time and efforts.

3.—The buyers were pleased with their purchase, and received a decided satisfaction in its possession.

4.—Readers of the book were gratified to see their author clothed in such fitting and harmonious dress.

5.—Reading the text has instructed some, and possibly inspired a few to nobler thinking.

❧ After "The Defense of Guinevere" was published, it was thirteen years before Morris issued another volume. His days had been given to art and the work of management. But now the business had gotten on to such a firm basis that he turned the immediate supervision over to others and took two days of the week, Saturday and Sunday, for literature.

Taking up the active work of literature when thirty-seven years of age, he followed it with the zest of youth for twenty years—until death claimed him ❧ William Morris thought literature should be the product of the ripened mind—the mind that knows the world of men and which has grappled with earth's problems. He also considered that letters should not be a profession in itself—to make a business of an art is to degrade it. Literature should be the spontaneous output of the mind that has known and felt. To work the mine of spirit as a business and sift its product for hire, is to overwork the vein and palm off slag

WILLIAM MORRIS for sterling metal. Shakespeare was a theatre manager, Milton a secretary, Bobby Burns a farmer, Lamb a book-keeper, Wordsworth a government employee, Emerson a lecturer, Hawthorne a custom-house inspector and Whitman a clerk. William Morris was a workingman and manufacturer,—and would have been Poet Laureate of England had he been willing to call himself a student of sociology instead of a socialist. Socialism itself (whatever it may be) is not offensive—the word is.

NCE upon a day the great American Apostle of Negation expressed a regret that he had not been consulted when the Universe was being planned, otherwise he would have arranged to make good things catching instead of bad.

The remark tokened a slight lesion in the logic of the Apostle, for good things are now, and ever have been, infectious.

❧ Once upon a day, I met a young man who told me that he was exposed at Kelmscott House for a brief hour, and caught it, and ever after there were in his mind, thoughts, feelings, emotions & ideals that had not been there before. Possibly the psychologist would explain that the spores of all these things were simply sleeping, awaiting the warmth and sunshine of some peculiar presence to start them into being; but of that I cannot speak—this only I know, that the young man said to me, "Whereas I was once blind, I now see."

❧ William Morris was a giant in physical strength and a giant in intellect. His nature was intensely masculine in that he could plan & act without thought of precedent. Never was a man more emancipated from the trammels of convention and custom than William Morris.

Kelmscott House at Hammersmith is in an ebb-tide district where once wealth and fashion held sway; but now the vicinity is given over to factories, tenement houses and all that train of evil and vice that follow in the wake of faded gentility.

At Hammersmith you will see spacious old mansions used as warehouses; others as boarding-houses; still others converted into dance halls with beer gardens in the rear, where once bloomed and blossomed milady's flower beds.

⚓ The broad stone steps and wide hallways and iron fences, with glimpses now and then of ancient doorplates or more ancient knockers, tell of generations lost in the maze of oblivion.

Just why William Morris, the poet and lover of harmony, should have selected this locality for a home is quite beyond the average ken. Certainly it mystified the fashionable literary world of London with whom he never kept goose-step, but that still kept track of him—for fashion has a way of patronizing genius—and some of his old friends wrote him asking where Hammersmith was, and others expressed doubts as to its existence. I had no difficulty in taking the right train for Hammersmith, but once there no one seemed to have ever heard of the Kelmscott Press. When I inquired, grave misgivings seemed to arise as to whether the press I referred to was a cider press, a wine press or a press for "cracklings."

Finally I discovered a man—a workingman—whose face beamed at the mention of William Morris. Later I found that if a man knew William Morris, his heart throbbed at the mention of his name, and he at once grew voluble and confidential and friendly. It was the "Open Sesame." And if a person did not know William Morris, he simply did n't, and that was all there was about it.

But the man I met knew "Th' Ole Man," which was the affectionate title used by all the hundreds & thousands who worked with William Morris. And to prove that he knew him, when I asked that he should direct me to the Upper Mall, he simply insisted on going with me. Moreover, he told a needless lie and declared he was on the way there, although when we met he was headed in the other direction. By a devious walk of half a mile we reached the high iron fence of Kelmscott House. We arrived amid a florid description of the Icelandic Sagas as told by my new-found friend & interpreted by Th' Ole Man. My friend had not read the Sagas, but still he did not hesitate to recommend them; and so we passed through the wide open gates and up the stone walk to the entrance of Kelmscott House. On the threshold we met Mr. F. S. Ellis & Mr. Emery Walker, who addressed my companion as "Tom." I knew Mr. Ellis slightly & also had met Mr. Walker, who works Rembrandt miracles with a camera. Mr. Ellis was deep in seeing the famous "Chaucer" through the press, and Mr. Walker had a print to show, so we turned aside, passed a great pile of paper in crates that cluttered the hallway, and entered the library. There, leaning over the long, oaken table, in shirtsleeves, was the master. Who could mistake that great, shaggy head, the tangled beard, and frank, open-eyed look of boyish animation?

The man was sixty & more, but there was no appearance of age in eye, complexion, form or gesture—only the whitened hair! He greeted me as if we had always known each other, and Ellis and piles of Chaucer proof led straight to old Professor Child of Harvard, whose work Ellis criticised and Morris upheld. They fell into a hot argument, which was even continued as we walked across the street to the Doves Bindery ✍

The Doves Bindery, as all good men know, is managed by Mr. Cobden-Sanderson, who married one of the two daughters of Richard Cobden of Corn-Law fame ✍✍✍

Just why Mr. Sanderson, the lawyer, should have borrowed his wife's maiden name and made it legally a part of his own, I do not know. Anyway, I quite like the idea of linking one's name with that of the woman one loves, especially when it has been so honored by the possessor as the name of Cobden.

Cobden-Sanderson caught the rage for beauty from William Morris, and began to bind books for his own pleasure. Morris contended that any man who could bind books as beautifully as Cobden-Sanderson should not waste his time with law. Cobden-Sanderson talked it over with his wife, and she being a most sensible woman, agreed with William Morris. So Cobden-Sanderson, acting on the suggestion of Th' Ole Man, rented

the quaint and curious mansion next door to the old WILLIAM
house occupied by the Kelmscott Press, and went to MORRIS
work binding books.

When we were once inside of the Bindery, the Chau-
cerian argument between Mr. Ellis and Th' Ole Man
shifted off into a wrangle with Cobden-Sanderson. I
could not get the drift of it exactly—it seemed to be
the continuation of some former quarrel about an oak
leaf or something. Anyway, Th' Ole Man silenced his
opponent by smothering his batteries—all of which
will be better understood when I explain that Th' Ole
Man was large in stature, bluff, bold and strong-voiced,
whereas Cobden-Sanderson is small, red-headed,
meek, and wears bicycle trousers.

The argument, however, was not quite so serious an
affair as I at first supposed, for it all ended in a laugh
and easily ran off into a quiet debate as to the value
of Imperial Japan vs. Whatman.

We walked through the various old parlors that now
do duty as workrooms for bright-eyed girls, then over
through the Kelmscott Press, and from this to another
old mansion that had on its door a brass plate so polished and repolished, like a machine-made sonnet too
much gone over, that one can scarcely make out its
intent. Finally I managed to trace the legend, "The
Seasons." I was told it was here that Thomson, the
poet, wrote his book ✌ Once back in the library of
Kelmscott House, Mr. Ellis and Th' Ole Man leaned
over the great oaken table and renewed, in a gentler

21

WILLIAM MORRIS key, the question as to whether Professor Child was justified in his construction of the Third Canto of the "Canterbury Tales." Under cover of the smoke I quietly disappeared with Mr. Cockerill, the Secretary, for a better view of the Kelmscott Press.

This was my first interview with William Morris. By chance I met him again, some days after, at the shop of Emery Walker in Clifford Court, Strand. I had been told on divers occasions by various persons that William Morris had no sympathy for American art and small respect for our literature. I am sure this was not wholly true, for on this occasion he told me he had read "Huckleberry Finn," and doted on "Uncle Remus." He also spoke with affection and feeling of Walt Whitman, and told me that he had read every printed word that Emerson had written. And further he congratulated me on the success of my book, "Songs from Vagabondia."

THE housekeeping world seems **WILLIAM** to have been in thrall to six **MORRIS** hair-cloth chairs, a slippery sofa to match, and a very cold, marble-top center table, from the beginning of this century down to comparatively recent times. In all the best homes there was also a marble mantel to match the center table; on one end of this mantel was a blue glass vase containing a bouquet of paper roses, and on the other a plaster-Paris cat. Above the mantel hung a wreath of wax flowers in a glass case ✱ In such houses were usually to be seen gaudy-colored carpets, imitation lace curtains, and a what-not in the corner that seemed ready to go into dissolution through the law of gravitation. ✱ Early in the seventies lithograph presses began to make chromos that were warranted just as good as oil paintings, and these were distributed in millions by enterprising newspapers as premiums for subscriptions. Looking over an old file of the "Christian Union" for the year 1871, I chanced upon an editorial wherein it was stated that the end of painting pictures by hand had come, and the writer piously thanked heaven for it—and added, "Art is now within the reach of all." Furniture, carpets, curtains, pictures and books were being manufactured by machinery, and to glue things together and give them a look of gentility & get them

23

WILLIAM MORRIS into a house before they fell apart, was the seeming desideratum of all manufacturers.

❧ The editor of the "Christian Union" surely had a basis of truth for his statement; art had received a sudden chill: palettes and brushes could be bought for half-price, and many artists were making five-year contracts with lithographers; while those too old to learn to draw on lithograph stones saw nothing left for them but to work designs with worsted in perforated cardboard.

To the influence of William Morris does the civilized world owe its salvation from the mad rage & rush for the tawdry and cheap in home decoration. It will not do to say that if William Morris had not called a halt some one else would, nor to cavil by declaring that the inanities of the Plush-Covered-Age followed the Era of the Hair-Cloth Sofa. These things are frankly admitted, but the refreshing fact remains that fully one-half the homes of England & America have been influenced by the good taste and vivid personality of one strong, earnest man.

William Morris was the strongest all 'round man the century has produced. He was an Artist and a Poet in the broadest and best sense of these much bandied terms. William Morris could do more things, and do them well, than any man of either ancient or modern times whom we can name.

William Morris was master of six distinct trades. He was a weaver, a blacksmith, a wood-carver, a painter,

24

a dyer and a printer; and he was a musical composer of no mean ability.

⚓ Better than all, he was an enthusiastic lover of his race: his heart throbbed for humanity, and believing that society could be reformed only from below, he cast his lot with the toilers, dressed as one of them, and in the companionship of workingmen found a response to his holy zeal which the society of an entailed aristocracy denied.

The man who could influence the entire housekeeping of half a world, and give the kingdom of fashion a list to starboard; who could paint beautiful pictures; compose music; speak four languages; write sublime verse;
address a public assemblage effectively; produce
plays; resurrect the lost art of making books
—books such as were made only in the
olden time as a loving, religious ser-
vice; who lived a clean, whole-
some, manly life—beloved by
those who knew him best
—shall we not call
him Master?

SO HERE ENDETH THE LITTLE JOURNEY TO THE
HOME OF WILLIAM MORRIS, AS WRITTEN BY ELBERT
HUBBARD, THE TITLE PAGE AND INITIALS BEING
DESIGNED BY ROYCROFT ARTISTS AND THE WHOLE
DONE INTO A PRINTED BOOK BY THE ROYCROFTERS,
AT THEIR SHOP, WHICH IS IN EAST AURORA, NEW
YORK, IN THE MONTH OF JANUARY, IN THE YEAR MCM